I0157631

DEDICATED TO...
THE YOUTH LEADERSHIP CONFERENCE
FOR COMMUNITY PROGRESS

THE COURAGE TO MARCH:
THE AMAZING TRUE STORY OF REVEREND R.A. CALLIES

Copyright © 2025, Arlington Callies

All rights reserved. No part of this book may be reproduced, distributed, or transmitted in any form or by any means, or stored in a database or retrieval system, without the prior written permission of the publisher. The only exception is brief quotations in printed reviews.

ISBN# 979-8-9925783-2-4

For information and permission requests, contact:
VC Publishing
PO Box 536
Argyle, TX 76226
info@VinsonCS.com

For interviews and
booking information contact:
Arlington Callies
New Home Realty, LLC
arlington@newhomerealtytx.com
210-860-5381

THE COURAGE TO MARCH

THE AMAZING TRUE STORY OF REVEREND R.A. CALLIES

BY: ARLINGTON CALLIES

VC
PUBLISHING

Rev. Callies loved spending time with his family, especially when they took long road trips to Arkansas. They laughed and shared stories together.

Rev. Callies loved sharing stories about God's love.
He preached and taught with so much joy!
He wanted everyone to know how amazing God is.

Besides being a preacher,
Rev. Callies was also a carpenter!
He founded and built two amazing
churches from the ground up.

And guess what? He was a teacher, too! Rev. Callies taught woodshop at Martin Luther King, Jr. Middle School.

He helped kids
create all kinds of
cool things.

After school the kids wanted to play, but there was a problem. They didn't have a park to play football in. So, they played in the streets instead and it wasn't very safe.

Rev. Callies thought, "wouldn't it be nice if the kids had a safe place to play?"

He had a big idea! Let's make our community safer and more fun for everyone.

He gathered his neighbors and shared his big idea: "We can build a park for the kids! We can have sidewalks and traffic lights to keep people safe, and even a street named after Dr. Martin Luther King, Jr.!"

Leaders in the community loved his ideas, and encouraged him to talk to the mayor and the city council.

So, Rev. Callies did just that! He asked the mayor and city council to build a park with all the things they wanted. He even asked them to rename a street after Martin Luther King, Jr.

But the city council said "No!"

Rev. Callies didn't give up. He gathered his neighbors and organized a March! They carried signs and marched through the streets, asking for the things their community needed.

The city council saw how important it was to the people and finally agreed! Rev. Callies and his community were so happy!

But Rev. Callies had another dream! He told the community he wanted to build a big statue of Martin Luther King, Jr. in the park to inspire everyone who saw it.

The city loved his idea, but they didn't have enough money. Rev. Callies didn't give up. He decided to get the young people involved. He started the Youth Leadership Conference for Community Progress (YLCCP)!

Every Saturday, YLCCP members asked for donations to help build the statue of Dr. King. They worked hard all Spring and Summer long.

NEW HOME REALTY

All their hard work paid off, they raised enough money! The whole community came together to celebrate the statue of Dr. Martin Luther King, Jr. in their park.

And guess what? The March Rev. Callies started kept growing year after year! Today, San Antonio has the biggest Martin Luther King, Jr. march in the whole country...

All thanks to Rev. Callies
and his big dreams!

Rev. Callies' courage reminds us of Martin Luther King Jr.'s words: "Faith is taking the first step even when you don't see the whole staircase." Rev. Callies took that first step for his community, and because of that, amazing things happened!

It's Coloring Time!

The following pages are just for you!
You can color the pictures any way you like.
There are no right or wrong colors—only your colors.
Have fun, take your time, and let your imagination run wild!

www.ingramcontent.com/pod-product-compliance
Lightning Source LLC
Chambersburg PA
CBHW042106040426
42448CB00002B/160